AF269504

CHINESE MYTHOLOGY

Guandi
God of War

BY SAMANTHA S. BELL

CONTENT CONSULTANT
GANG LIU, PhD
ASSOCIATE TEACHING PROFESSOR
CARNEGIE MELLON UNIVERSITY

Kids Core
An Imprint of Abdo Publishing
abdobooks.com

abdobooks.com

Published by Abdo Publishing, a division of ABDO, PO Box 398166, Minneapolis, Minnesota 55439. Copyright © 2023 by Abdo Consulting Group, Inc. International copyrights reserved in all countries. No part of this book may be reproduced in any form without written permission from the publisher. Kids Core™ is a trademark and logo of Abdo Publishing.

Printed in the United States of America, North Mankato, Minnesota.
102022
012023

Cover Photo: Germán Vogel/Moment/Getty Images
Interior Photos: Pictures from History/Universal Images Group/Getty Images, 4–5, 16; Album/Alamy, 6; Ratchakrit Nakkhonok/Alamy, 9; Georg Westermann/Antiqua Print Gallery/Alamy, 10; Shutterstock Images, 12–13, 18, 20–21, 24, 28 (top), 29 (top); Heritage Images/Hulton Archive/Getty Images, 14, 28 (bottom); Paul Rushton/Alamy, 22, 29 (bottom); Martin Malchev/Alamy, 26

Editor: Ann Schwab
Series Design: Ryan Gale

Library of Congress Control Number: 2022940684

Publisher's Cataloging-in-Publication Data

Names: Bell, Samantha S., author.
Title: Guandi: God of War / by Samantha S. Bell
Description: Minneapolis, Minnesota: Abdo Publishing, 2023 | Series: Chinese Mythology | Includes online resources and index.
Identifiers: ISBN 9781532199943 (lib. bdg.) | ISBN 9781098275143 (ebook)
Subjects: LCSH: Deities--Juvenile literature. | Gods, Chinese--Juvenile literature. | Mythology, Chinese--Juvenile literature.
Classification: DDC 299.51--dc23

CONTENTS

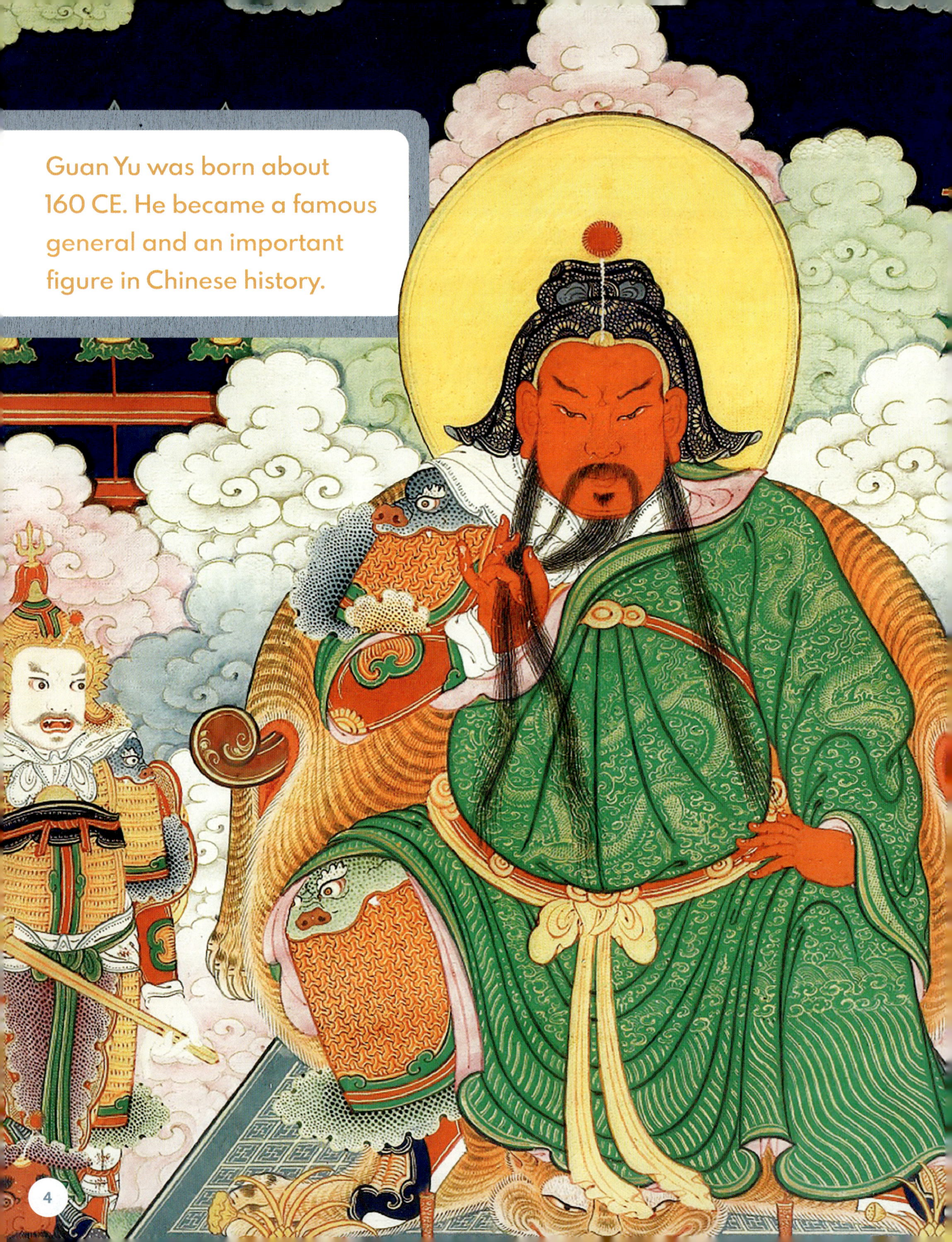

Guan Yu was born about 160 CE. He became a famous general and an important figure in Chinese history.

CHAPTER 1

The Protector

Guan Yu always had a sense of justice, even as a young man. One day, he heard an old man and a young woman crying. Guan Yu asked them what was wrong. The old man said the young woman was his daughter.

In art, Guan Yu is often shown with a red face.

She was engaged to be married. But the uncle of the local official had seen how beautiful she was. He wanted to marry her instead. The father asked the official to help them, but he refused.

Guan Yu became very angry. He grabbed a sword and killed the official and the official's uncle. Military officers chased Guan Yu, but he escaped. Then he stopped by a brook to wash his face. As he did so, his face changed color to become reddish gray. Guan Yu returned, but the officers did not recognize him.

When Guan Yu grew up, he became a famous warrior. He was strong and fierce, but he was also very loyal and **honorable**.

He was so honorable that after he died, he became a god named Guandi. He is known as the god of war. But he tries to prevent wars. He wants to protect people from the terrors of war.

Combining Myths with History

There are many stories about Guan Yu. Some of them are true. Guan Yu was an important

The Three Kingdoms

After the Han **dynasty** fell in 220 CE, China was divided into three kingdoms: Wei, Shu, and Wu. Known as the Three Kingdoms Period, it was a time of constant warfare. The kingdoms had separate rulers. Guan Yu had fought for two of these leaders during the collapse of the Han dynasty.

figure in Chinese history. He was born about 160 CE and died in 219 or 220 CE, when the Han **dynasty** was collapsing. He lived just before the period of the Three Kingdoms (220–280 CE). Guan Yu served in many battles as a skilled military general.

Three Kingdoms Map

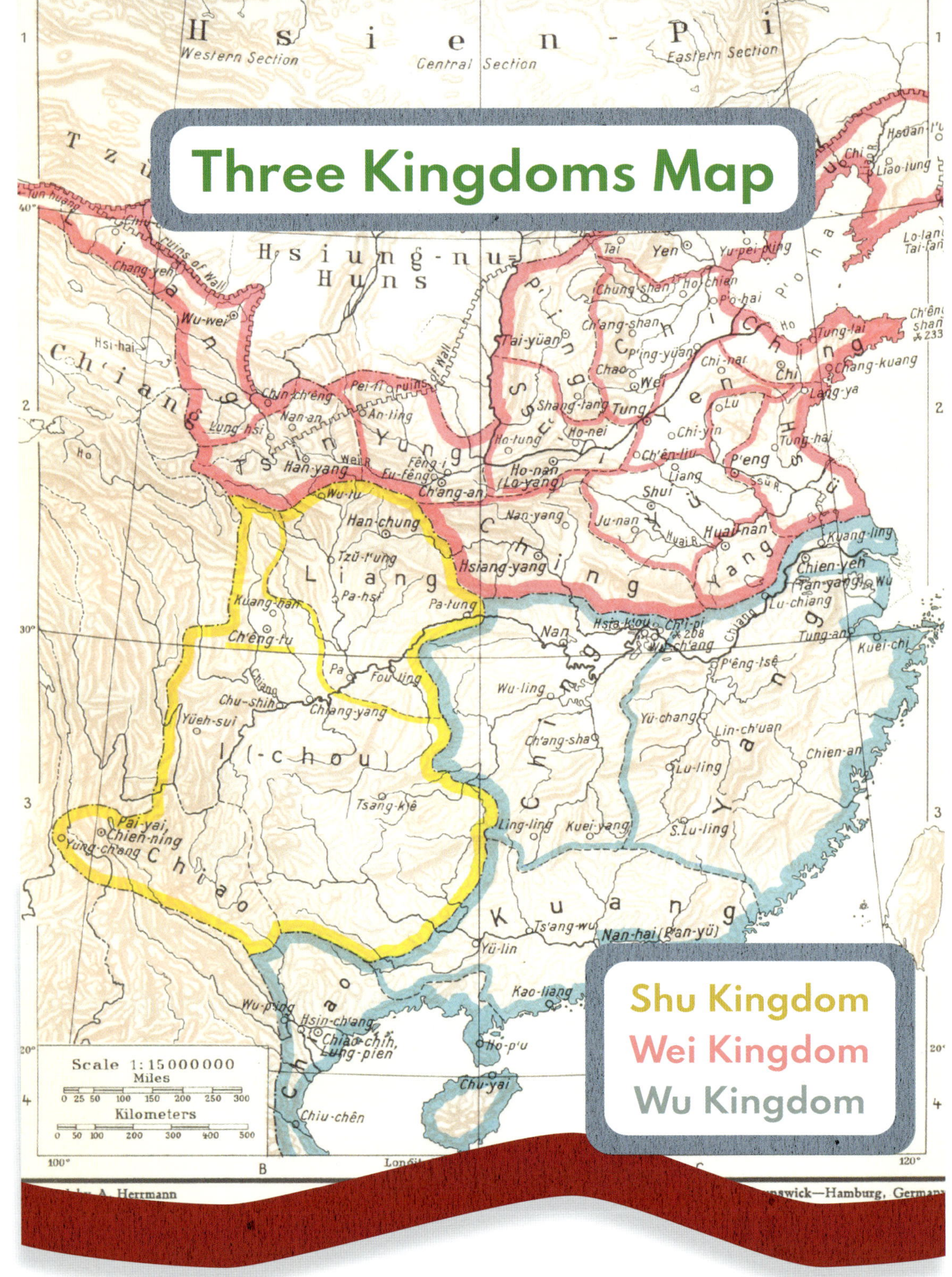

China was split into three separate kingdoms from 220 to 280 CE. As these regions were forming, Guan Yu served the men who would become rulers of the Shu and Wei Kingdoms.

After Guan Yu died and became Guandi, he also became the god of war, wealth, and literature. Many myths have been told about him. Chinese myths are stories, legends, and folktales that have been passed down for centuries. Many of them are about gods and goddesses. Myths about Guandi were written in books or performed as plays. Over time, more stories were added.

Explore Online

Visit the website below. Does it give any new information about Guan Yu that was not in Chapter One?

Guan U or Guan Yu

abdocorelibrary.com/guandi

Guan Yu, *right*, was a fearless warrior.

Family Bonds

Some of the stories about Guan Yu include his family members. Guan Yu's youngest son was named Guan Xing. He never missed his target with a bow and arrow. Guan Xing later became a military leader like his father.

Liu Bei, Guan Yu, and Zhang Fei, *left to right*, took an oath of brotherhood in a peach orchard.

Brothers by Choice

Some stories say that Guan Yu ran away from home. He decided to join the army. On his way, he met two men, Liu Bei and Zhang Fei. Liu Bei was from a royal family. He wanted to defeat the **rebels** that had taken over the land. Zhang Fei was a butcher from a village. He wanted to help Liu Bei restore peace. Guan Yu decided to help too. The three men went to Zhang Fei's peach orchard. They took an **oath** of brotherhood. They promised to always help each other and serve their country.

Guan Yu's mighty horse, Red Hare, was his loyal companion on the battlefield.

Liu Bei eventually became the ruler of one of the Three Kingdoms. But Guan Yu and his oldest son, Guan Ping, were captured and killed by the enemy. Liu Bei's family built a temple for Guan Yu to show how thankful they were. Later, other rulers did the same. Guan Yu became China's most well-known military hero.

The Great Horse

A ruler once gave Guan Yu a horse called Red Hare. It was the best gift Guan Yu ever received. It could run 258 miles (416 km) in a day. After Guan Yu was killed, it is said that Red Hare refused to eat. It died grieving its master.

Mighty Powers

People believe that Guandi, as a god, continues to fight for what is right. He is the guardian of justice for all people, no matter their position or status. Guandi can send rain when the people need it. He has healing powers for the sick.

As the god of war, Guandi only uses violence to help people. In some stories, his spirit soldiers help the human armies. Today, many soldiers are still his loyal followers.

Primary Source

In the 1300s, Luo Guanzhong wrote a novel in which he describes Guan Yu, Liu Bei, and Zhang Fei taking the oath of brotherhood:

> We will rescue each other in difficulty; we will aid each other in danger. We swear to serve the state and save the people.

Source: Luo Guanzhong. *Romance of the Three Kingdoms*. Tuttle, 2002, p. 8.

Comparing Texts

Think about the quote. Does it support the information in this chapter or give a different perspective? Explain your answer in two or three sentences.

Guandi is honored by all believers, not just soldiers.

CHAPTER 3

A God for All People

People believe that Guandi helps all people, no matter their class or occupation. Some of the people he helps are city **merchants**. He helps them make more money.

Businesses often display a statue of Guandi. It is
believed he will help bring wealth and success.

Guandi also created a method for them to keep track of the money they make. For these reasons, Guandi is also known as a god of wealth. Like the soldiers, the merchants appreciate Guandi's skills, honesty, and loyalty.

People in villages worship Guandi too. They think of him as the provider for and protector of their communities. Thousands of temples have been built throughout China to honor Guandi. Many people still greatly respect him today as the god who brings success to businesses. Restaurant owners often place a statue of Guandi in a small **shrine**.

A gigantic statue of Guandi towered above Jingzhou, China. In 2021, workers began moving it to a nearby city.

Guandi is also the protector of temples. Some myths tell about a demon that began threatening a temple. The priest called on Guandi for help. Guandi sent his spirit soldiers, and they fought and defeated the demon.

Guandi in Art

In sculptures and paintings, Guandi usually has a long beard and a red face. His red face represents loyalty and justice. Some stories describe him as having bushy eyebrows like silkworms. Others say he has the eyes of a **phoenix**.

Epic Warrior, Epic Statue

Sculptures of Guandi are still created today. The largest one stands 157 feet (48 m) high. It was originally built in 2016 in Jingzhou, in south-central China. But residents of that city thought it was too big. In 2021, workers began moving it to a nearby city where Guan Yu is believed to have trained his troops.

A fierce warrior, Guan Yu used a dangerous weapon in battle.

Guan Yu stood about 7.2 feet (2.2 m) tall. He usually carried a weapon called a *guan dao*.

It had a long handle with a large curved blade on the end.

To some people, Guandi is the loyal warrior. To others, he is a hero who protects their temples and their homes. To still others, he is the provider of wealth and health. Guandi means different things to different people. But they all believe that he is a god who is on their side.

LEGENDARY FACTS

Guan Yu was a fierce and strong warrior.

He swore an oath with Liu Bei and Zhang Fei to support each other and serve their country.

After he died, he
became Guandi,
the god of war.

People believe that
Guandi controls the
rain, keeps temples
safe, and helps
businesses succeed.

Glossary

dynasty
a series of rulers from the same family

honorable
honest and worthy of respect

merchants
people who sell goods

oath
a vow or promise

phoenix
a mythological bird that dies in a fire but rises again from the ashes

rebels
people who fight against the established government of their country

shrine
a sacred place or object that is dedicated to a god

Online Resources

To learn more about Guandi and Chinese mythology, visit our free resource websites below.

Visit **abdocorelibrary.com** or scan this QR code for free Common Core resources for teachers and students, including vetted activities, multimedia, and booklinks, for deeper subject comprehension.

Visit **abdobooklinks.com** or scan this QR code for free additional online weblinks for further learning. These links are routinely monitored and updated to provide the most current information available.

Learn More

Hamby, Zachary. *Introduction to Mythology for Kids.* Rockridge, 2020.

Yip, Mingmei. *Chinese Children's Favorite Stories: Fables, Myths, and Fairy Tales.* Tuttle, 2020.

Index

About the Author

Samantha S. Bell lives in the foothills of the Blue Ridge Mountains with her family and lots of cats. She is the author of more than 130 nonfiction books for kids.